POWER YOUR MIND

Tools to Build Resilience

RI | RECOVERY INTERNATIONAL
BETTER. MENTAL. HEALTH. ™

Recovery International
Oak Brook, IL

Power Your Mind: Tools to Build Resilience (Revised Edition)

Copyright ©2023 Recovery International

All rights reserved. No portion of this workbook may be reproduced, stored in a retrieval system, or transmitted in any form or by any means—electronic, mechanical, photocopy, recording, scanning or other—except brief quotations in critical reviews or articles, or as specifically allowed by the US Copyright Act of 1976, without the prior written permission of the copyright owner.

Published by: Recovery International
1415 W. 22nd Street – Tower Floor
Oak Brook, IL 60523
RecoveryInternational.org

ISBN: 978-1-7342697-9-6

Interior Design: Odd Duck/B. Quellos

Illustrations by Charad Perkins, Chris O'Connell & Ryan Vila

Printed in the United States of America

TABLE OF CONTENTS

INTRO 1

PART 1 Temper Has Two Faces 3

PART 2 Environment Has Two Faces 9

PART 3 Building Resilience 13

PART 4 The 4-Step Method 19

PART 5 Stopping, Thinking, Action Tools 25

PART 6 Humor & Facing Our Fears 31

PART 7 Group Minded vs. Self-Focused 37

CONCLUSION 41

GLOSSARY OF TERMS 42

EXAMPLE WORKSHEET 44

This workbook is designed to be used as a self-help program or as part of a group training session. While the Recovery International Method often serves as an adjunct to professional care, it is not a substitute for therapy, counseling or medical advice or treatment. This program focuses on dealing with everyday events and situations that may cause you stress. If you are experiencing a serious or traumatic situation, please contact a trusted adult or a mental health or health care professional or call 988.

www.PowerYourMind.org
info@poweryourmind.org

INTRODUCTION

Welcome to Power Your Mind: Tools to Build Resilience, a guide for young adults seeking new tools to better cope with the stress of everyday living.

Little things can add up. Maybe we are running late to meet friends, or we flunked an exam, or something was posted about us on social media. Maybe we are having a REALLY bad day and it is everything at the same time. When these situations happen, they can leave us feeling irritated, upset, or sad.

When little things add up, it can lead to feelings of anxiety, anger, or depression. We may lose our temper or start feeling bad. It can spin out of control fast, making the situation worse, leaving us hurt and confused.

Power Your Mind is based on a program that has helped tens of thousands of individuals around the world better cope with events that trigger symptoms and negative feelings. It's a proven method to help us handle situations that are confusing or upsetting.

This is a self-paced guide to work through on your own or as part of a group. Each section presents tools to use to deal with everyday stress and upsets. In the pages ahead, we will learn:

- That there are two sides to our temper and what we can do about each side.
- How to recognize situations outside of our control and better manage our inner thoughts and emotions.
- Lots of tools to deal with situations as they arise.
- The 4-Step Method for handling an event.
- And much more!

You will find plenty of opportunities to put these lessons to the test! We'll show examples of these ideas in action then offer tips to use them. Based on programs we have run before, we suggest completing one section per week; that allows time to think about new terminology and to gain practice using these tools in everyday life. In order to get the most out of this program, we need to give ourselves the chance to truly learn and practice these tools.

Before we dive into our first lesson, think about what you want to accomplish by the time you finish this guide. Look at how this program has helped others on the next page.

Testimonials

"We have peace in our family today, and my family trusts me again." — Antonio

"I can see the viewpoints of others and am less sensitive to criticism." — Sara

"I don't know what I would do without this program. I had no tools to deal with my anxiety, and was barely functioning until I started learning the method." — Louise

"I think before I speak. I get less irritated and angry. I am more self-forgiving." — Lily

"This has changed my life. It has helped me grow as a person. I learned how to cope with my nervous symptoms and it taught me how to change my thoughts and see my anxiety differently." — Brendan

"It has helped me feel less anxious and more in control of my thoughts. I behave better. My family and friends notice and they find many of the tools very useful for themselves." — Tamika

ACTIVITY

Set a personal goal.

Circle some words or phrases in these testimonials that resonate with you. Write a statement for yourself that reads like these success stories. What do you want to improve? What would you like to say about yourself one day?

_____
_____
_____
_____
_____
_____

In the weeks ahead, refer back to this page. Look at your goal and consider how you are making progress.

Part 1
TEMPER HAS TWO FACES

There are two kinds of tempers.

Angry Temper is when we feel wronged by someone else. For example, a friend stands us up, we get cheated out of a deal, someone else gets us in trouble, or we get snubbed outright. These situations can leave us feeling irritated, resentful, disgusted, or impatient.

Fearful Temper is when we feel we are in the wrong. For example, we get confused about what time we are supposed to meet someone and show up late, we joke at a party and hurt someone's feelings, or we answer a question wrong and get called out by the teacher. As a result, this can leave us feeling bad about ourselves. We start to worry, experience feelings of shame and fear, or feel hopeless.

> **IN THIS SECTION YOU WILL DISCOVER:**
>
> 1. Temper has two faces: Angry & Fearful
> 2. "Judgment" is an element of both
> 3. Tools we can use to control our temper

With Angry Temper, we are judging that another person has wronged us. We may not have all the facts or know the details, but we feel that we are right, and they are wrong, and we act accordingly. We get angry when we think other people are wrong or have wronged us.

With Fearful Temper, we judge ourselves as being wrong. This can make us feel self-conscious, inadequate, or ashamed.

Judgment is one thing that both types of temper have in common.

If we could all learn to drop the judgment, we could avoid distress. But it's not quite that simple.

FEARFUL TEMPER

The judgment that **I am wrong**

Feelings related to Fearful Temper:
- WORRY
- FEELING OF INADEQUACY
- HOPELESSNESS
- FEAR OF DAMAGE TO MYSELF OR MY REPUTATION
- SENSE OF SHAME

Can you think of more?

ANGRY TEMPER

The judgment that the **other person is wrong** or has wronged me

Feelings related to Angry Temper:
- IRRITATION
- RESENTMENT
- IMPATIENCE
- HATRED
- DISGUST
- REBELLION

Can you think of more?

HERE IS THE THING...

We can't control how other people act. We can't really control other people at all. We can't control events or circumstances or situations. We can only control ourselves—and how we respond to these things. If we think others are wrong, we get angry or rebellious. If we think we are wrong or others think we are wrong, we worry, feel inadequate, and feel worthless.

But we can change our reactions by controlling our thoughts and impulses. This program teaches us how. It begins by knowing the difference between angry and fearful temper.

Let's see if we can spot the temper in Max's story on the next page.

MEET MAX

Max is waiting outside the theater for his friend.

Terri is LATE! We're gonna miss the start of the movie.

I'm really STEAMED!

Meanwhile in Max's mind.....

Max is pretty angry. How can we help him turn his frustration into something positive?

Maybe he doesn't have to blame or accuse anyone. He can control the way he acts. Maybe he can see the other side of the story.

Let's see how Max handles the situation.

I don't know why she's late.

Maybe she's stuck in traffic or something.

I just have to RELAX...

There's a few shows in the next 40 minutes. We can catch one if she's really late.

REFLECT

1. Describe Max's situation.
2. Can you tell which kind of temper (angry or fearful) Max is experiencing?
3. What does Max seem to be feeling?

If you said that Max was exhibiting an Angry Temper—getting irritated and impatient with Terri—you are correct. Put yourself in Max's shoes. Do you think he may have also experienced Fearful Temper?

ACTIVITY #1

Angry Temper: Describe a time when you thought another person was wrong and you were right. Be brief. Focus on what you were feeling. What were your thoughts about the other person? Did you have any physical reactions to temper?

_____
_____
_____
_____
_____
_____

In Max's situation, we saw that he was able to get his angry temper under control.
- Can you identify three ways that Max was able to keep his anger in check?
- What did Max do to drop the judgment of his friend?
- How was he able to take control of the situation?

By recognizing that he didn't know both sides of the story, Max was able to manage his reaction. In addition, by identifying the situation as something relatively common and average (or trivial), he was able to not take it personally, instead of assuming Terri was late on purpose to irritate him. He managed to calm down, and also found alternative solutions if Terri arrived too late to make the first show.

On the next page are some tools Max used, as well as other tools for managing angry temper that he could have used. As you read them, see which apply to Max's situation.

Some Tools for Angry Temper

- We can learn to express our feelings without temper.
- We excuse rather than accuse ourselves and others.
- Humor is our best friend; temper is our worst enemy.
- We can choose peace over power.
- It takes two to fight, one to lay down the sword.
- If we can't change a situation, we can change our attitude toward it.
- We can drop the judgment for the sake of our mental health.
- Feelings should be **expressed** and temper **suppressed**.
- Every act of self-control leads to a greater sense of self-respect.
- People do things **that** annoy us, not necessarily **to** annoy us.
- We can remove ourselves from a tense situation.
- Temper keeps us from seeing the other side of the story.

Now let's look at the situation you wrote out earlier. Look at the event you listed and try to create a positive outcome (even if it didn't end that way) by using some of the tools listed above.

Choose **three** tools from this list and apply them to your own situation.

1. How could the outcome have been different using these tools?
2. How could you use these tools the next time you are in a similar situation to achieve a positive outcome?
3. What tools on the list are you committed to trying next time? Circle them. You could also take a picture of the tools on your phone for quick access.

ACTIVITY #2

Fearful Temper: Describe a time when you thought you might be wrong. Focus on what you were feeling. What were your thoughts about yourself? Did you have any physical reactions to temper?

_____
_____
_____
_____
_____

Now, let's look at ways you could have changed this situation or taken control of it for yourself. Here is a list of tools for fearful temper. As you read through the list, imagine how you could use these tools in your situation.

> **Some Tools for Fearful Temper**
> - Humor is our best friend; temper is our worst enemy.
> - We learn not to take ourselves too seriously.
> - Symptoms are distressing, but not dangerous.
> - Helplessness is not hopelessness.
> - Temper maintains and intensifies symptoms.
> - Fear is a belief and beliefs can be changed.
> - We can accept or reject thoughts that come to us.
> - Decide, plan and act.
> - When feeling overwhelmed, do things in "part acts"—one step at a time.

Choose **three** tools from this list and apply them to your own situation.

1. How could the outcome be different using these tools?
2. How could you use these tools the next time you are in a similar situation?
3. Choose one or two tools on the list and commit to trying them the next time you are in a stressful situation.

REVIEW

Now that you have finished this section, you should be able to:

1. Tell the difference between the two types of temper.
2. Recognize Angry and Fearful Temper in your own experiences.
3. Identify some tools for each type of temper and have a plan to use them.

Part 2
ENVIRONMENT HAS TWO FACES

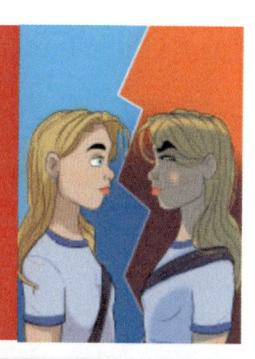

We can't control what our friends or family do. We can't control our partner or significant other. We can't control the guy on the bus or the woman in the car. No matter how much we want them to behave a certain way—it is, quite literally, out of our hands, or beyond our fingertips and **out of our control**.

This is what we call our **external environment**. We may want something to happen—to make the team, get a part in a school play, or land that job—but once we've done our part (try out, audition, or interview), those things are out of our control and in the hands of others.

IN THIS SECTION YOU WILL DISCOVER:

1. Environment has two faces: Internal & External
2. The difference between the two
3. What you can and can't control

This is also true for accidents, world events, or things we see online. Finally, **we can't control the past** any more than we can control people or events. History is beyond our fingertips. Whatever has happened— experiences in childhood or memories— these things are outside of our control. It's over, even if we think about them once in a while.

ACTIVITY #1

Look around and name three things you see in the **external** environment that you CAN'T control.

_____

_____

_____

Our **internal environment** is everything we **can control**. But this can be tricky. We can't control our initial feelings and sensations during an event. If something happens and we feel scared and start to sweat or feel flush in the face, that's not controllable. However, what happens next can be controlled. We have thoughts about the situation such as "Why did he have to prank me?" And we may have the impulse to run away or yell. These **thoughts and impulses can be changed and controlled.**

Name three things that are in your **internal** environment that you CAN control.

_____

_____

_____

ACTIVITY #2

Look at this list of **feelings, impulses, sensations,** and **thoughts** and place them in the chart. You can remember these with the acronym **FIST**.

- Anger
- Tightness (muscles)
- Fear
- To sulk
- "I am worthless."
- Love
- Excitement
- To complain
- Sweating
- To yell
- Racing heartbeat
- To hit
- Hatred
- Embarrassment
- Tenseness
- "I will never amount to anything."
- Adrenaline rush
- To overeat.
- "This is dangerous to my reputation."
- Breathing faster
- To run away
- To avoid doing something
- "They are wrong."
- Jealousy

Now, add at least one feeling, impulse, sensation, and thought that you have experienced in the last day—positive or negative—to the chart.

Can't Control | Can Control

Feelings
Initial emotional reactions

Impulses
Strong, sudden wish to do something

Sensations
Physical responses or perception

Thoughts
Ideas, plans, opinions you think

MEET TERRI

Terri is on her way to meet Max. She is running late. Max is probably going to be upset with her. Check out what is going through her head as she sits in traffic.

ARRGGH!

I'M SO LATE!

THESE DRIVERS ARE **IDIOTS**!

I SHOULDN'T HAVE TAKEN THIS ROAD.

Now IN TERRI'S MIND.....

TERRI IS WORKED UP. BUT THIS IS AN AVERAGE SITUATION.

SHE CAN'T CHANGE THE SITUATION, BUT SHE CAN CHANGE HER ATTITUDE TOWARD IT. COMFORT IS A WANT NOT A NEED.

THERE'S NO NEED TO STRESS OR FEAR DANGER.

I CAN'T CHANGE BEING IN THIS STUPID TRAFFIC...

BUT I DON'T NEED TO STRESS. I'LL BE FINE.

SINCE I'M STOPPED, I'LL JUST CALL MAX. I'M ALMOST THERE, ANYWAY.

WE CAN CATCH A LATER SHOW.

REFLECT

1. Describe Terri's situation.
2. What is external and out of her control?
3. What is in Terri's internal environment (or in her control)?

Terri can't control the time, the traffic, other drivers on the road, or whether or not Max is mad at her. We've all been there, right? We are going to meet a friend, heading to practice, or running late for class, and everything feels overwhelming. We make the situation worse by giving into our emotions and getting worked up. What Terri **can** control is how she responds to other people and events. She feels anxious and frustrated, but she smooths things out by applying her tools and taking action. She acknowledges what is not in her control and recognizes what is.

Now, let's combine the concepts of **temper and environment**. Look at Max's situation. He was angry. He also could have been insecure, thinking that Terri didn't care about him enough to be on time. By recognizing his inner feelings of **angry** or **fearful** temper and **using tools**, Max changed his thoughts, stayed calm, and gained control.

When we feel anxious about an everyday situation that we can't get out of—like Terri stuck in traffic—we can **spot angry temper** (frustration at others). Then using the tools, "If we can't change a situation, we can change our attitude towards it" and "We can take a secure thought that it won't last forever," we take control of the situation.

The same situation could turn into **fearful temper** by accusing ourselves with thoughts like, "I should have left the house earlier" and "I shouldn't have come this way." Again, this is a time to remember tools like, "I spot that it is average to get caught in traffic," "These symptoms are distressing but not dangerous," or "Drop the judgment."

By using tools, we can calm ourselves and realize that bad traffic or being late to the movies are trivial, average events—they are not emergencies. There may also be reasons we are not aware of yet: our friend may have had a flat tire, or lost track of time, or traffic may have been slow. We can change our reactions and our plans and still enjoy time together.

REVIEW

We learned some valuable lessons on how to deal with everyday experiences and average events without losing our cool. Now, you should be able to:

1. Recognize there are two faces of environment: internal and external.
2. Tell the difference between them and recognize what you can control.
3. Apply tools to what is in your control and let go of the rest.

Part 3
BUILDING RESILIENCE

Resilience is the ability to bounce back, stay calm, and recover quickly. Most things that upset us are little things. If we learn to manage our responses to life's trivial events, we'll cope better and stay calm. And we'll be better able to handle big challenges when they arise.

Will
Remember we can only control our thoughts and impulses. We cannot control other people or a situation. In this chapter, we are going to talk about the most important thing there is to control: ourselves. Being able to control our actions, thoughts and impulses—that's our will and will-power.

IN THIS SECTION YOU WILL DISCOVER:

1. How to recognize Trivialities
2. The 3 Ps for developing our Will
3. The meaning of Self-Endorsement and putting it into practice

By controlling our reactions, we can often influence the outer environment and others. For example, when we use tools to drop our temper, our calm reaction can help calm the reactions of those around us.

The tools in this program will help us act and think differently than before. If we practice them again and again, then everyday annoyances or common situations—trivialities—will not bother us as much. And when you do that, you deserve a pat on the back—or a **self-endorsement.**

The 3Ps for Developing Our Will
Think of will-power like a muscle. Strengthening your will builds resilience. In the same way that you make yourself stronger by lifting weights, faster by running, or more flexible by doing yoga—we can have more self-control by exercising our will.

We exercise our will through 3Ps: Perseverance. Patience. Perspective.

- The will to **persevere:** finding a way to keep going when we feel beat down and sticking with something until it's finished.
- The will to **patience**: finding a "pause" button and stopping our impulse to react.
- The will to get **perspective**: considering how severe the situation is and choosing how to think or respond.

TRIVIALITIES
Most things that upset us are the routine events in everyday life.

YOUR WILL
You have the power to choose:

- How you are going to act
- What you are going to think

SELF-ENDORSEMENT
You deserve a mental pat on the back for any effort:

- To spot your temper
- To control your thoughts and impulses

Trivialities are average events that most people experience. They are common. They are not moral, legal, or ethical issues, but they are little things that can get us worked up. They do not require police, firefighters, doctors, or other emergency professionals.

For example, what we choose to wear to school, make a wrong turn, or wait longer than expected for our food order. They are not right or wrong, they just happen. We give them value with our thoughts, emotions, and actions. We can choose how we respond to them. We can let them get us worked up or we can let them go.

Some Tools for Trivialities

- Expectations can lead to disappointments.
- People do things **that** annoy us, not necessarily **to** annoy us.
- Treat life as a business, not as a game.
- Do the thing you fear and hate to do, as long as there is no danger.
- Try, fail; try, fail; try, succeed.
- You can't control the outer environment.
- The outer environment can be rude, crude and indifferent.
- Have the courage to make a mistake in the trivialities of everyday life.
- If we can't change a situation, we can change our attitude toward it.
- There is no right or wrong in the trivialities of everyday life.

MEET CHERYL

Cheryl is shopping at the mall when she sees a friend. She calls out, but her friend doesn't respond.

The local mall.

"Hey, Angie! It's me, Cheryl. Over here. Wait up!"

"Now, son... you just bought two figures.."
"This party's gonna be cool!"
"Agreed!"
"Can't wait!"
"DAAAAAAD!! Please..."

Awwww, man. Angie's ignoring me... She didn't even turn around.

Meanwhile in Cheryl's mind.....

"Cheryl should think of the **situation**."
"It's pretty **noisy** at the mall."
"And it looks like Angie was in a **conversation** with her friends."

"It's ok."
"They probably didn't hear me. The kid was **extra loud**, and she was talking to her friends."
"I'll catch up with her another time."

Page 15

REFLECT

Cheryl could have felt angry, blaming others for making so much noise that her friend didn't hear her. Or she could have felt upset (fearful temper) thinking that her friend might have ignored her on purpose. Either way, she might be feeling bad—wanting to yell or tear up.

Instead, she used tools to recognize this wasn't a big deal. She couldn't control the situation—it was noisy—and she excused her friend for not hearing her. Instead of yelling louder and making a scene, she shrugged it off and went on her way.

Trivialities are everywhere. Think of Terri stuck in traffic, thinking to herself: "I shouldn't have taken this road." She is blaming herself (fearful temper) for taking the "wrong way" and blaming others (angry temper) for making the traffic so heavy. These things are trivial. Her judgments give them value—negative value, in this case.

ACTIVITY #1

Evaluate your day.
Start from the time that you woke up until this moment. Think of all the small events that happened between then and now. Did you eat breakfast? Did you get dressed? Did you talk to a friend? Did you read a social media post? All these actions were trivial.

Write them out and note how significant they seemed at the time by rating each one from 1 to 10 (mild to intense).

_____ 1 2 3 4 5 6 7 8 9 10

_____ 1 2 3 4 5 6 7 8 9 10

_____ 1 2 3 4 5 6 7 8 9 10

_____ 1 2 3 4 5 6 7 8 9 10

_____ 1 2 3 4 5 6 7 8 9 10

Now, look over the list of tools and see if any of them could have helped change your attitude or rating about these trivial events.

ACTIVITY #2

Will-Power: Below are tools for building our will. Check at least three you'd like to practice using this week.

Some Tools for Will

- We can decide which thoughts to think.
- We can decide which words to use.
- We can decide which actions to take.
- Do things in part acts—one step at a time.
- Every act of self-control leads to a greater sense of self-respect.
- Feelings and sensations cannot be controlled, but thoughts and impulses can.
- Replace an insecure thought with a secure thought.
- Try, fail; try, fail; try, succeed.
- There are no uncontrollable impulses, only impulses that are not controlled.
- If we can't decide, any decision will steady us.

Endorsing: Below are tools for self-endorsing. List three things you can endorse yourself for doing this past week.

Tools for Endorsing

- When you are endorsing yourself, you can't be blaming yourself.
- Endorse yourself when you spot your temper.
- We can decide which actions to take.
- Endorse yourself when you control your thoughts.
- Endorse yourself when you control your impulses.
- Congratulate yourself for the effort, not the outcome.

_____

_____

_____

Choose at least three endorsements you'd like to practice using this week.

ACTIVITY #3

So far, we've met Max, Terri, and Cheryl and learned how they handled common daily situations (trivialities). Now let's think about ways each character **persevered,** had **patience,** or had **perspective**.

- Which character(s) **persevered** despite their situations? How did they show perseverance?
- Which character(s) practiced **patience**? In what way?
- Which character(s) had **perspective** that their situation wasn't a big deal?

Fill in the chart.

Perseverance	Patience	Perspective

REVIEW

In this section, we unpacked the meaning of "will-power" and learned that, in the same way that exercise builds muscle, there are ways to develop our will and make it stronger. As we conclude this section, we should know how to:

1. Recognize ways to navigate the trivialities of everyday life.
2. Identify the 3Ps to *Develop our Will*: perseverance, patience, and perspective.
3. Congratulate ourselves for small efforts and accomplishments.

Part 4
THE 4-STEP METHOD

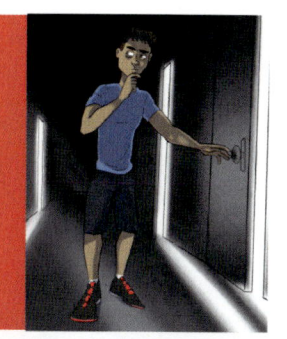

The 4-Step Method teaches us to **report a situation rather than complain about it** and work it up. It allows us to identify what we are feeling and use the tools from this book to drop the judgment of ourselves or others.

IN THIS SECTION YOU WILL DISCOVER:

1. The 4-Step Method for Taking Control
2. Identifying an Event
3. Recognizing Your Symptoms
4. Influencing an Outcome

Step 1 begins with an **event.**

An event is an objective experience. It is what actually occurs without our thoughts, impressions, and judgments getting in the way. Remember, in the last section, when we talked about trivialities, we recognized that experiences are only "good" or "bad" when we apply judgment to them.

An event is composed of who was there, what was said, actions that were taken, and the time and place of the experience. It is everything that goes into an experience without our own perspectives layered into the event.

When we are taking the first step in the process, we describe "just the facts" of the event, without adding embellishments or feelings. We end this step with "that's when I worked myself up."

Step 2 in this process involves the **symptoms** we experience.

If we post something to social media and we get negative comments or only a few shares or "likes," we may start to get worked up, our heart might pick up its pace, or we may feel tension in our jaw or fists. These are symptoms triggered by the event. Our feelings, sensations, thoughts, and impulses (racing heart, tight jaw, sweaty palms, etc.) are all symptoms. Identifying those is a way to know we are getting worked up.

Step 3 is **spotting.**

This goes back to the first chapter: noticing our temper. Is it angry or fearful? Spotting is shining a spotlight on something—such as identifying our temper and figuring out what tools we need to get our symptoms under control. We can identify the parts of the external or internal environment that influences the event.

What **tools** can we use? Identify the tools (listed in previous chapters) that help us drop the judgment. How can we look at the situation without letting things get out of control?

Step 4 is the **outcome**.

This is a way of looking at the situation with different outcomes. Imagine what the situation looks like when we put our tools in action vs. the way it looked when we didn't. If we notice a change, remember to endorse for that!

Before we learned and started practicing with the tools, our symptoms and emotions were running the show. Maybe we lost our temper when we felt insulted. Perhaps a misunderstanding led to an avoidable situation where we got in a fight with a friend and stopped talking for weeks. Now, the same situation— when we apply tools—plays out differently.

ACTIVITY #1

Let's apply the 4-Step Method to Max's situation.

Step 1 - Describe an everyday event that got you worked up. What triggered temper and symptoms?

Max: I was waiting for a friend, and she was late. That's when I worked myself up.

Step 2 - Report the symptoms you experienced, both physical and mental.

Max: I was clenching my jaw; my face was getting flushed. I was thinking angry thoughts, saying angry words.

Step 3 - Report your fearful and angry temper, the tools you used, and self-endorsement.

Max: I had fearful temper that she didn't want to be with me, that she didn't care to show up. I was in angry temper that she kept me waiting. I spotted that I should excuse, not accuse, that I shouldn't take it personally—maybe she couldn't help it. I endorsed for realizing I could control my reaction.

Step 4 - Describe what would have happened before this training—your reaction or discomfort—and endorse for your effort or any improvement.

Max: Before this, I would have yelled at her when she got there, and we would have fought. It would have ruined the whole night. Now, I can relax and figure out a Plan B.

Now, we invite you to spot. Look at the tools for **Angry Temper** (page 7). What other tools do you think Max could have used?

_____

_____

_____

Max also admits he had fearful temper—that Terri might have decided not to show up. Look at the tools for **Fearful Temper** (page 8). What other tools do you think Max could have used?

_____

_____

ACTIVITY #2

How would the **4-Step Method** apply in Terri's situation?

Step 1: **Describe** Terri's situation. Where is she? What is happening? What does the event look like objectively?

_____

_____

_____

Step 2: What were Terri's **symptoms**? What was she experiencing? What was she telling herself? What was happening emotionally? Physically?

_____

_____

_____

Step 3: **Spotting:** What kind of temper was Terri experiencing? What tools listed on pages 7, 8 or 14 did she use? Did she **endorse** herself?

_____

_____

_____

Step 4: **Outcome:** What would have happened before Terri used the tools she'd learned? What might have happened differently in her situation with Max if she didn't use tools?

___

ACTIVITY #3

Now, let's look at the **4-Step Method** with an example from your own life.

Step 1: Describe an upsetting situation. Where are you? What is happening? What does the event look like objectively?

___

Step 2: Report the discomfort you experienced right after the event—the first signs that you were in temper. What were your feelings, impulses, sensations, and thoughts in the example you gave? *(Did your heart race? Did your jaw clench? Did you feel like yelling or crying? Were you blaming yourself or someone else?)*

___

How would you rate your discomfort on a scale of 1 to 10? (mild to intense)

        Before Spotting: 1 2 3 4 5 6 7 8 9 10

Step 3: Spotting Temper, Tools and Endorsing
Angry or Fearful Temper —Did you feel someone else was wrong? Were you worried you were wrong? *Inner or Outer Environment* —Which parts of the situation were out of your control? Which parts could you control?

___

Look at the lists of **tools** on pages 7, 8 or 14, and write down which ones can help manage your reaction to this incident:

_____
_____
_____
_____
_____

What can you **endorse** for?

_____
_____
_____

Step 4: Describe what would have happened **before this training** and using the tools—the reaction and discomfort you would have experienced:

_____
_____
_____

Describe your reaction after using the tools in this program:

_____
_____
_____
_____
_____

Now rate your symptoms after using the tools on a scale of 1 to 10 (mild to intense).
   After Spotting: 1   2   3   4   5   6   7   8   9   10

Compare your "Before and After" scores and reactions.

Endorse yourself for your effort or any improvement!

Congratulations! You just completed your first 4-Step Method example.

REVIEW

We learned how to take control of ourselves and our actions by using the 4-Step Method.

As we conclude this chapter, you should know how to:

1. Consider an event objectively—relying on just the facts of the experience.
2. Recognize your symptoms—what we are feeling emotionally and physically.
3. Spot the right solution that will work in each situation.
4. Influence an outcome by considering how events might play out in response to different actions and reactions.

Use blank worksheets in the back of this book to write out more 4-Step Examples. Writing out examples helps us learn the 4-Step Method and the tools by heart. More downloadable worksheets and more tool lists can be found at **poweryourmind.org.**

Part 5
STOPPING, THINKING & ACTION TOOLS

The same tool can work in many different situations. Using humor, for example, can help with both fearful and angry temper. Laughing at ourselves is a way to cope with our internal environment and laughing at a situation is also a way to cope with external environment.

In this section, we look at three types of tools in a different way. Stopping, thinking, and action tools can be applied to a variety of situations, but they share a common thread as they teach our brain to either stop, think, or act.

IN THIS SECTION YOU WILL DISCOVER:

1. Stopping Tools
2. Thinking Tools
3. Action Tools
4. The Importance of Choice

Stopping Tools

Stopping Tools help us pump the brakes before we act or react to what we're feeling or experiencing. Stopping Tools are ways that we can hit pause between Steps 2 and 3 in the 4-Step Method. Let's say an event has occurred and we are experiencing symptoms of anger, are getting worked up, and are about to react.

Stopping Tools get us out of our thoughts, out of the story we are telling ourselves, out of the moment—so we can respond more appropriately.

Tools for Stopping

- Don't look regretfully into the past.
- Don't look fearfully into the future.
- Don't take yourself too seriously.
- Don't express anti-social responses.
- Don't accuse yourself or others.
- Don't express temper.
- Don't expect to be perfect.
- Don't try to please everybody.
- Don't try to control others.
- Don't dominate.

MEET GABRIELA

She wants to go to the game with her friends, and asks her mom for permission.

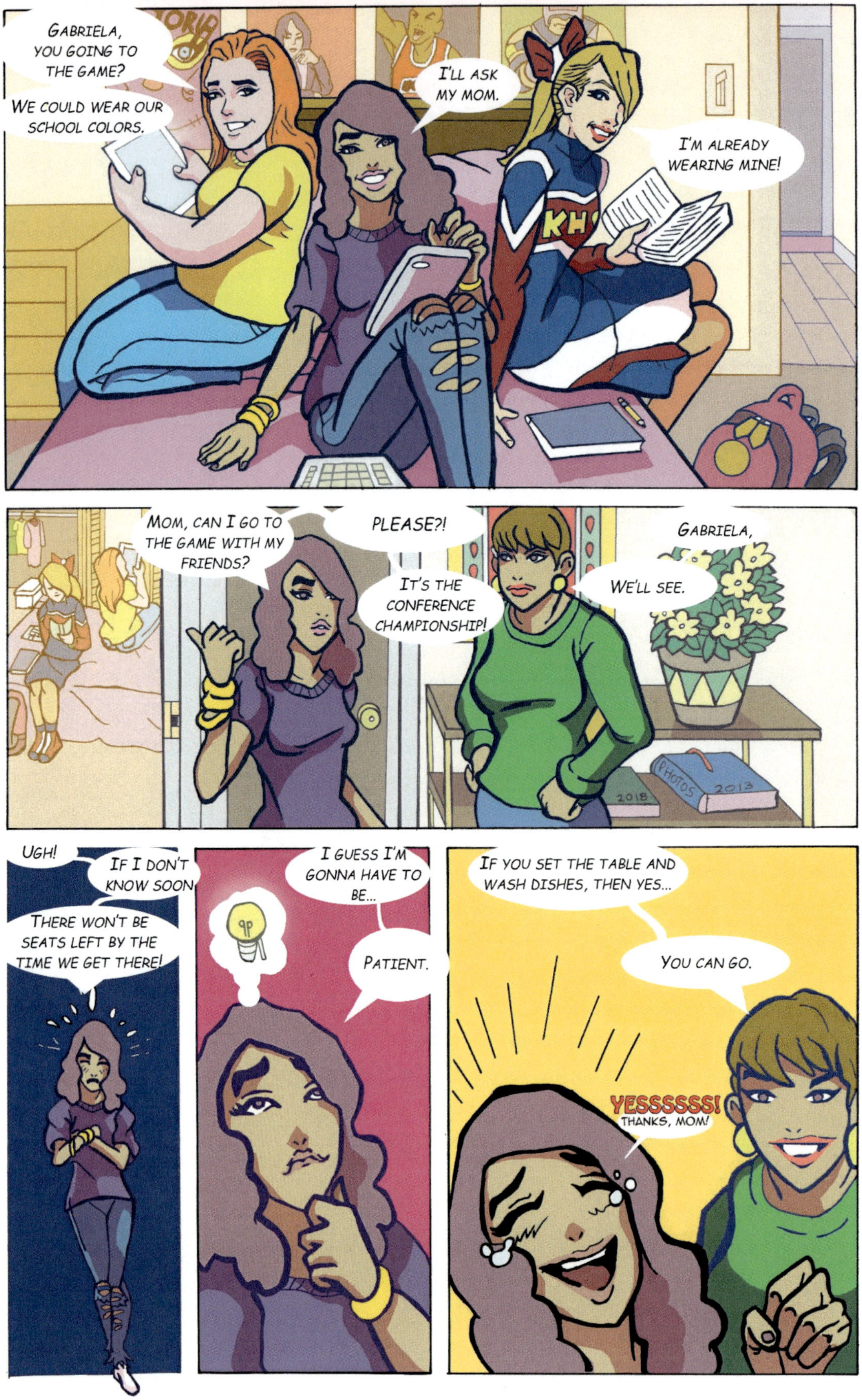

REFLECT

Gabriela's mother might have explained better when she would be able to give a more definite answer, or what Gabriela might be able to do to get a "yes" answer. That could have eased the frustration of not knowing. But "we can't control our outer environment," and Gabriela's mom is her outer environment. Stopping helps us choose whether to stay calm, make plans, or take action.

ACTIVITY #1

Even though you just learned these tools, you probably can think of a time when you should have stopped yourself from doing something. Note the situation and the tool (page 25) that could have helped.

I recall the time when:

_____

_____

I could have used the tool:

_____

Would the outcome have been better if you had chosen to stop?

Thinking Tools

Thinking tools help us realize there are different ways to look at things and that there are options when choosing the next step. Stopping allows us to choose how we want to act. Thinking tools give us more choices and opportunities to practice patience and perseverance.

Tools for Thinking
- Every act of self-control leads to a sense of self-respect.
- Expectations can lead to self-induced frustrations.
- Fear is a belief; beliefs can be changed.
- Fearful anticipation is often worse than the realization.
- Feelings and sensations cannot be controlled, but thoughts and impulses can.
- Helplessness is not hopelessness.
- Humor is our friend; temper is our enemy.
- It is ok to feel uncomfortable in an uncomfortable situation.
- Life is full of frustrations and irritations.

ACTIVITY #2

Write about a situation when you really wanted to say or do something, but decided not to or that it just wasn't worth it.

_____
_____
_____

Check the tool(s) that might apply to this example or find a previous tool that applies:
- o Every act of self-control leads to a sense of self-respect.
- o Feelings and sensations cannot be controlled, but thoughts and impulses can.
- o Frustrations are tolerable.
- o It takes two to fight, one to lay down the sword.

_____
_____

Think about a time when you were in an uncomfortable situation. What were the feelings and thoughts you experienced?

_____
_____
_____

Check the tool(s) that might apply to this example or find a previous tool that applies:
- o It is okay to feel uncomfortable in an uncomfortable situation.
- o Have the will to persevere.
- o Helplessness is not hopelessness.
- o Fear is a belief; beliefs can be changed.

_____
_____

Imagine what the outcome might have been like if you had used one of the tools.

Action Tools

Action Tools are positive thoughts, actions, or steps that we can choose. These are things we can start doing right now. Or, in a challenging situation, use these to influence the outcome. Action tools are a way to re-frame our thinking and to get our brain to move our muscles.

Tools for Action

- Anticipate joyfully.
- Assert yourself without temper.
- Be group-minded.
- Be self-led.
- Break old habits.
- Change to secure thoughts.
- Change your attitude to the situation.
- Control your mouth.
- Decide, plan and act.
- Decide which action to take.
- Decide which thoughts to think.
- Decide which words to use.
- Do things you don't like to do.
- Do things one step at a time.
- Endorse for each effort.
- Excuse others and yourself.
- Have the courage to make mistakes.
- Try fail; try fail; try succeed.

ACTIVITY #3

Write about a time when you had the courage to try something new even if you had doubts about your success.

_____
_____
_____

Check the tool(s) that might apply to this example:

- Have the courage to make mistakes in the trivialities of everyday life.
- Try fail; try fail; try succeed.
- Endorse for each effort.
- Decide, plan and act.

The Importance of Choice

Choice is the ultimate tool. It gives us the ability to act, react, or do neither. It allows us to control our thoughts. It influences outcomes. Choice is the ability to choose among the tools in our toolkit to take positive action.

If we are angry and about to yell at someone or hit them—**STOP! Don't move. Don't talk.** Think about what is going on. Decide whether or not to say something—work things out rather than work them up further.

On the other hand, if you are feeling a little nervous and you want reassurance—SPEAK UP! **Move your mouth and say something**—express what you want directly.

The graphic below shows how choice can influence the outcome. When something happens (an event), we react with feelings. These feelings create an impulse to act. We decide (with the power of choice) which action to take. We can choose to act with temper or with calm, with anger or with humor. We can choose to give in to where the impulse takes us, or we can apply one of the tools on the earlier lists.

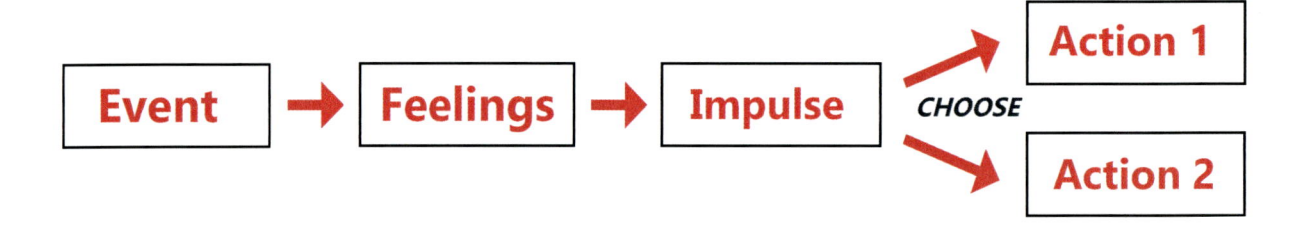

Event → Feelings → Impulse CHOOSE → Action 1 / Action 2

This process happens very fast.

The speed of event to emotion to action occurs in seconds…*whoosh*…or milliseconds. Remember, you have a choice which gives you power over this process.

REVIEW

In this section, we learned all the types of tools in our toolkit—Stopping Tools, Thinking Tools, Action Tools. As we conclude this section, you should know how to:

1. Use Stopping Tools to put the brakes on before you act, and prevent yourself from doing or saying something you might regret.
2. Use Thinking Tools to look at an event objectively and move out of the imaginative tale you are telling yourself. Look at things as they actually are.
3. Use Action Tools to move toward more positive outcomes that allow you to take action, shape your thoughts, and choose a good state of mind to move forward.

This week, practice using your three favorite tools from this chapter and use choice to create the space to influence outcomes.

Part 6
HUMOR & FACING OUR FEARS

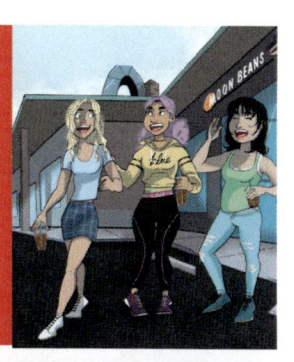

Now we are going to explore two more concepts: **Humor** and **Facing Your Fears**. Each concept will help us gain a deeper understanding of lessons presented so far.

IN THIS SECTION YOU WILL DISCOVER:
1. Humor Can Defuse Anger
2. How to Face Your Fears

Humor

If we have an outburst of temper and can see right away that the explosion is silly and laugh it off, then we are much less likely to have another outburst the next time we feel angry. Laughing it off relaxes us and gives us a way to defuse annoying incidents.

Humor isn't just about laughing—it can be an inner smile or a shrug. When we are in angry temper, try to shrug it off or find humor in the situation. When we are feeling fearful or insecure, use good humor to change our reaction.

ACTIVITY #1

Think of a time when you could have used humor to ease a tense situation.

_____
_____
_____
_____

What might have happened if you had used humor?

_____
_____
_____
_____

MEET JUAN

Juan has been practicing this program for more than six months. It has helped him control his anger so much that his family and friends have noticed.

REFLECT

Juan knows he has a short fuse. Being aware of this means that he can do something about it. He uses Stopping Tools and humor to deal with the situation.

Remember, spotting will helps us stay calm, take action or make plans when we use it in the moment, but it takes work. It is difficult. We need to train with this technique and practice until it becomes second nature.

Here is how Juan used the 4-Step Method in this situation:

Step 1: The Situation I saw a friend at the coffee shop, and said "hi," but he didn't hear me. I called out again and he yelled at me to leave him alone. That's when I worked myself up.

Step 2: Symptoms I got hot. I scowled and clenched my fists. I thought he was being rude on purpose. I had the impulse to yell at him.

Step 3: Spotting, Tools, and Endorsing I was in angry temper at him for his reaction. I was in fearful temper that he didn't like me. Then I spotted that it was sort of silly and it was trivial—no big deal. I used the tool "Every act of self-control leads to a sense of self-respect" and "Frustrations are tolerable" and "Humor is our best friend." I was proud of myself for not losing my cool. I endorsed for staying calm.

Step 4: Outcome Before, I would have yelled at him and told him off, and that would have been the end of our friendship. Now, I just shrugged and laughed it off.

What other Stopping tools could Juan have used? Check them below.

Tools for Stopping

- Don't look regretfully into the past.
- Don't look fearfully into the future.
- Don't take yourself too seriously.
- Don't express anti-social responses.
- Don't accuse yourself or others.
- Don't express temper.
- Don't expect to be perfect.
- Don't try to please everybody.
- Don't try to control others.
- Don't dominate.

Facing Your Fears

Remember, a fearful temper is often internally directed. When things aren't going our way or a situation doesn't work out the way we planned, we inflict damage on ourselves. It could be physical, emotional, or in the form of self-talk. Whatever way it is expressed, the bottom line is that when we feel uncomfortable, we often take it out on ourselves.

We might avoid sports practice after a particularly bad game because we feel judged and self-critical. We are bored with a new job, so we ditch work. We aren't grasping math, so we blow off the exam. Learning to play an instrument is hard, so we stop trying.

All these examples are "self-sabotage"—avoiding the discomfort. Facing our fears means going into the discomfort. It is not easy. It will be uncomfortable, challenging, scary, and awkward.

It is hard to go back to practice knowing that we lost the last game. It is difficult to put in the effort on a boring job when our friends are telling us to hang out with them. It is challenging to make ourselves study a subject or practice an instrument we don't enjoy. When we face our fears, we are better for it. The payoff isn't just overcoming that particular fear, but building a skill set that stays with us through the challenges and problems to come. It is a valuable lesson to learn from our fear.

Let's look at Gabriela's 4-Step Method:

Step 1: The Situation I wanted to go to the game with my friends, and asked my mom if it was okay. She said, "We'll see," and that is when I worked myself up.

Step 2: Symptoms I was upset. I pouted and worried I might not get to go. I wanted to cry and yell at her.

Step 3: Spotting, Tools, and Endorsing

I had angry temper at her because she didn't say "yes" right away. I had fearful temper that I would be the only one not able to go and my friends would think less of me. I spotted that I needed to be patient. I used the tools "You can't control your outer environment" and "I can't change the situation, but I can change my reaction to it." I endorsed for being patient.

Step 4: Outcome Before using my tools, I would have cried or yelled at her that she was not being fair. We would have fought and she would have grounded me. Instead, I waited and she let me know that if I helped with supper, then I could go to the game.

ACTIVITY #2

Think of a situation where you knew you were going to feel uncomfortable. Maybe you had to have a difficult conversation with a friend. Maybe you had to own up to a mistake you made, or go out of your comfort zone and speak in public. Maybe you had to tackle a project on a topic that's new to you. In these situations, we are forced to choose between avoiding our fears or facing them head on.

Write about a situation that happened in the past where you were afraid you would make a mistake or fail, but you did it anyway. Write how you successfully faced your fears and what the outcome looked like.

_____

_____

_____

_____

_____

_____

_____

_____

Now look forward to the future. Choose an event, experience, challenge or opportunity that you are afraid of tackling or feel uncomfortable doing. Use the 4-Step Method to help you get through it.

Step 1: The Situation

_____

_____

_____

Step 2: Your symptoms might be...

_____

_____

_____

_____

Step 3: Spotting, Tools and Endorsing Make a choice to face your fear, use some of your tools, and see how the situation works out. Don't forget to endorse for the effort, regardless of the outcome!

___

Step 4: Outcome Imagine what the outcome might be like if you apply your tools.

___

REVIEW

As with almost any skill, you get better at using it with practice. This is not just the end of the chapter, but the beginning of putting these tools to work for yourself. As we conclude this section, you should know how to:

1. Use humor as a tool to defuse anger.
2. Face your fears head on.

Part 7
GROUP MINDED VS. SELF-FOCUSED

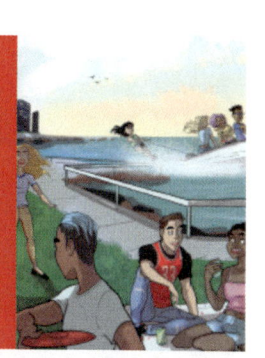

Congratulations!

You've reached the last chapter! What a journey it's been.

Group-mindedness is the last concept we want to introduce. It means service, self-control, and respect for the rights of others. It is also called **fellowship**.

We have spent time in previous chapters talking about how we cannot control others. We have discussed how trying often leads to frustration. When we feel out of control and cannot manage our own emotions, we sometimes look to control those around us, which doesn't work very well!

> **IN THIS SECTION YOU WILL DISCOVER:**
> 1. We are all part of many groups
> 2. The importance of being Group-Minded over Self-Focused
> 3. Tools for Group-Mindedness

The flip-side of being **self-focused** is group-mindedness: that is, respecting the autonomy and interests of the group, separating ourselves and our own wants and needs.

Group-mindedness is different from peer pressure, where you may feel pressured to behave how other members of the group want you to. Group-mindedness is about respecting the interests of the group, consistent with your own values. You have the power to make the choices that feel right to you.

There are many types of groups. Some may be loosely connected—like a crowd at a concert—or they may be close-knit, like a family. All kinds of different groups exist in the range between the crowd and the family, with varying degrees of fellowship.

A group of friends should have more fellowship than a group of students in a class at school, and the group of students in a class at school should have more fellowship than a group of strangers at a town meeting.

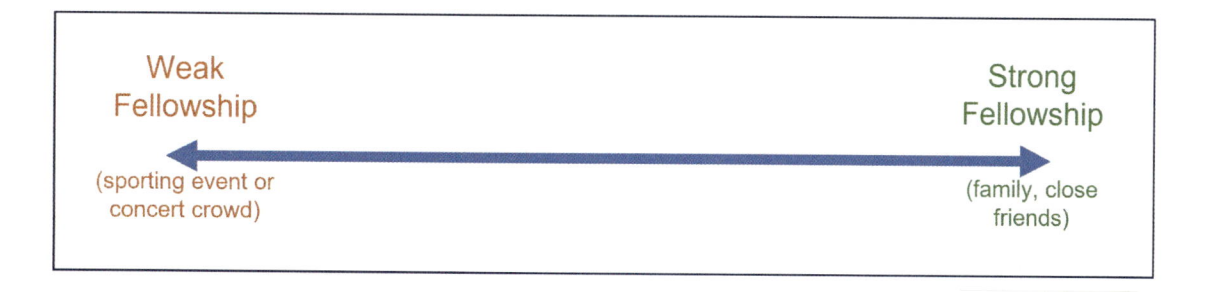

Weak Fellowship ←—————————————→ Strong Fellowship
(sporting event or concert crowd)   (family, close friends)

MEET ROBERT

Robert has a lot on his mind. But when his mother asks him to run an errand, he's group-minded enough that he agrees, even if reluctantly.

Panel 1: THE STATE CHAMPIONSHIP IS COMING UP... I GOT THREE TESTS AND A BIG ART PROJECT... AND MOM WANTS ME TO GET BREAD!! IT'S NOT FAIR...

Panel 2: HEY, I CAN'T BELIEVE YOU'RE HANGING OUT WITHOUT ME. SORRY, BUT DEB AND I WERE GOING TO WORK ON A... OH

Panel 3: FORGET IT!

Panel 4: HE SEEMS STRESSED. THAT'S UPSETTING. HE'S USUALLY CHILL... AND THE NICEST GUY.

Panel 5: (Robert fuming)

Panel 6: MAN, I SHOULDN'T HAVE BEEN A JERK TO MY GIRLFRIEND. SHE HAD OTHER PLANS AND HER OWN LIFE. ROBERT, TURN AROUND. PSST!

Panel 7: TAMIKA! I'M SORRY I TREATED YOU LIKE THAT AND IN FRONT OF YOUR FRIEND, TOO. I SHOULDN'T LET MY STRESS CONTROL MY IMPULSES. THANK YOU. IT'S HARD TO BALANCE EVERYTHING GOING ON. IT'S GOOD YOU WALKED AWAY...BUT NEXT TIME, LET'S TALK ABOUT IT.

REFLECT

Before this program, Robert might have snapped at his mother for asking him to run an errand, but he agreed to do it for the sake of the family group. People often forget the spirit of fellowship with their family and closest friends—temper is common in many families.

The same is true with partners. That's what Robert did at first. He expected Tamika to come with him—he didn't ask about her plans or invite her to join him.

We can reduce temper and have more peace by spotting that it is not necessary to dominate or compete, and that it is helpful to be of service and be group-minded at home and with friends.

ACTIVITY #1

Think of all the groups to which you belong. Include your family, your school, your class, and your community. List clubs, teams, organizations, and jobs.

_____   _____

_____   _____

_____   _____

_____   _____

Are there different expectations for how you act in each group? To put it another way, do you act differently in school than when you are with your friends? How about when you are with your teammates as opposed to a family meal?

Some Tools for Group-Mindedness

- Don't take yourself too seriously.
- Be group-minded, not self-focused.
- People do things **that** annoy us, usually not **to** annoy us.
- Group-importance is favored over self-importance.
- Home should be a domain of service and cooperation.
- The feeling of fellowship gives rise to the will to peace.
- The will to peace makes for understanding; the will to power makes for misunderstanding.
- Balance group needs with individual needs, desires and values.

Here is Robert using the 4-Step Method:

Step 1: The Situation I was going to the store to get some bread for my mom, and I ran into my girlfriend and her friend. I wanted her to come with me, but she didn't want to. That's when I worked myself up.

Step 2: Your Symptoms I said "Forget it!" and stalked off. I was angry. I was clenching my jaw and fists. I was thinking angry thoughts and had the impulse to break up with her.

Step 3: Spotting, Tools and Endorsing I spotted angry temper at Tamika for not saying "yes" right away. I spotted fearful temper that maybe she didn't want to be with me because I was being demanding and not inviting her to come along. I realized I was taking my frustration of having to run an errand out on my girlfriend. I used the tools "Feelings and sensations cannot be controlled, but thoughts and impulses can" and "We excuse rather than accuse ourselves and others." I endorsed for realizing this was trivial and I calmed down.

Step 4: Outcome Before this program, I would have dwelled on my anger. I would have felt that she had wronged me—not that I had done anything wrong. I would have kept expecting her to drop everything when I showed up. Now I am able to see her side, that she might have had plans with her friend, and that she didn't like me acting that way towards her. Now we can plan a better time to get together that works for both of us.

REVIEW

As we conclude this section, you should know how to:

1. Apply Group-Mindedness in various situations.
2. Avoid being Self-Focused.
3. Have respect for the rights of others.

This week, pay special attention to all the different groups to which you belong. Do you treat your family differently than your friends? Do you treat people you know differently than those you just met? Think about ways to maintain peace within each group. Endorse for each effort to find balance in your groups and in your life.

CONCLUSION

Congratulate yourself! You completed the **Power Your Mind** program! Hopefully this journey has been helpful, interesting, and informative. Most importantly, we hope you have picked up some useful tools and skills:

- tools to help with challenges and trivialities
- tools to help manage your emotions, control your impulses, and handle events as they arise
- tools to **stop** negative thoughts and reactions, to **think** about what is going on, and to **do** something different that will make things better.

IN THIS SECTION YOU WILL DISCOVER:
1. Your progress on your goal
2. Glossary of Terms
3. 4-Step Method worksheets

Habits we develop early on help us now and years down the road. The tools might pop into our heads when we least expect them, and help us manage a tricky situation!

Finally, let's go back to page 2 where you started the session by looking over some of the success stories from other participants and developing your own personal goal. Circle the rating that best describes how much progress you feel you have made toward that goal.

| 1 | 2 | 3 | 4 | 5 | 6 | 7 | 8 | 9 | 10 |

No progress   Much progress

Endorse yourself for the effort you put toward that goal!

Keep this book handy in the weeks and months to come. Revisit the exercises. Use new tools. Rework the activities. Try them out. Apply new tools to your life each time you work through this material.

For more information on resources or to find Tools and 4-Step Method templates, go to **poweryourmind.org**

Thank you! And again, congratulations!

GLOSSARY OF TERMS

> Our program uses terms that have specific meaning—sometimes the meaning may be a little different than how these words are typically used. Using these words signals our brain that we are thinking differently and that we are changing our thought patterns by using tools to stay calm.

Angry Temper: Negative judgments directed against another person or situation (i.e. they are wrong). This can take the form of resentment, impatience, indignation, annoyance, irritation, disgust, hatred or rebellion.

Averageness: Most of daily life consists of average experiences that everyone faces. It is helpful to set realistic goals and not expect perfection.

Bad Habits: Destructive behaviors that we do habitually and carelessly (i.e. crying habit, complaining habit, gossiping habit, sarcasm habit).

Drop the judgment: Using tools to change reactions, relieve tension, reduce anxiety or temper, or become calm.

Fearful Temper: Negative judgments directed against oneself (i.e. I am wrong). This can take the form of discouragement, preoccupation, worry, embarrassment, hopelessness or despair.

Feelings: Emotions such as anger, impatience, hatred, fear, worry, embarrassment, shame, and many more. We cannot control our initial feelings.

Good Habits: Endorsing, using our tools, exercising, being group-minded, etc.

Group-minded: Thinking about what is best for our group (i.e. family, classmates, friends, etc.).

Impulses: What we first want to do, such as to punch, to run, to hug, to laugh, to yell, and so on. We can learn to control our impulses.

Inner Environment: Everything inside oneself including feelings, sensations, thoughts and impulses.

Outer Environment: Everything outside oneself, including people, the weather, traffic, events and the past.

Sabotage: Anything done to interfere with the goal of managing anger and fear, such as using temperamental language, not using the tools, or rebelling. When we ignore or choose not to practice what we have learned. When we do not do what is best for our mental health.

Self-endorsement: A mental "pat on the back" or self-praise for effort in practicing the method, using tools, and controlling thoughts and impulses; recognizing the value of every effort made regardless of the result.

Self-focused: Asserting individual rights and domination over someone else.

Sensations: Physical responses such as blushing, racing heartbeats, tense muscles, teary eyes, and many more. You cannot control these initial sensations.

Spotting: Identifying a disturbing feeling, sensation, thought or impulse; then applying the tools. Understanding the underlying meaning of words or events, and using tools to react.

Symptoms: Thoughts or physical reactions to fearful or angry temper (i.e., lethargy, agitation, increased heart rate).

Temper: Caused by judging right and wrong in minor, everyday events. (Note: This does not apply to legal, moral, or ethical issues.)

Temperamental deadlock: Quarreling over who is right and who is wrong in everyday situations—it doesn't matter! It becomes an angry standoff.

Temperamental language: Exaggerated, negative, or insecure descriptions of experiences. All language that is alarming and defeating.

Thoughts: Ideas produced by thinking, such as, "This is fun," "I can do this," "He is annoying," and so on. You can learn to change your thoughts.

Tools: Short sentences or phrases that are used as reminders of the techniques and concepts we are learning and practicing.

Trivialities: The routine events and irritations of daily life. Most events are trivial when compared to the importance of our health (mental, spiritual, emotional, and physical).

Vicious cycle: Temper and tenseness that increase the length and intensity of negative feelings and sensations.

Will: The power to choose how you are going to act and what you are going to think.

Working ourselves up: When we take negative or distressing thoughts and impulses and escalate them.

EXAMPLE WORKSHEET

Step 1: Report a situation—an everyday event when you began to work yourself up. Describe what happened: specifically, what triggered temper and symptoms?

_____
_____
_____

Step 2: Report the symptoms you experienced—both physical and mental. (For instance, angry and fearful thoughts, confusion, tightness in your chest, low feelings, sweaty palms, and so on.)

_____
_____
_____

How would you rate your discomfort on a scale of 1 to 10? (1=mild through 10=very intense)

Before Spotting: 1 2 3 4 5 6 7 8 9 10

Step 3: Report your spotting of fearful and/or angry temper, the RI tools you used to help yourself, and self-endorsement for your effort.

_____
_____
_____
_____

Step 4: Describe what would have happened before your training—the reaction and discomfort you would have experienced—and rate your discomfort after spotting.

_____
_____
_____
_____

After Spotting: 1 2 3 4 5 6 7 8 9 10

Endorse yourself for your effort and any improvement!

EXAMPLE WORKSHEET

Step 1: Report a situation—an everyday event when you began to work yourself up. Describe what happened: specifically, what triggered temper and symptoms?

_____
_____
_____

Step 2: Report the symptoms you experienced—both physical and mental. (For instance, angry and fearful thoughts, confusion, tightness in your chest, low feelings, sweaty palms, and so on.)

_____
_____
_____

How would you rate your discomfort on a scale of 1 to 10? (1=mild through 10=very intense)

Before Spotting: 1 2 3 4 5 6 7 8 9 10

Step 3: Report your spotting of fearful and/or angry temper, the RI tools you used to help yourself, and self-endorsement for your effort.

_____
_____
_____

Step 4: Describe what would have happened before your training—the reaction and discomfort you would have experienced—and rate your discomfort after spotting.

_____
_____
_____

After Spotting: 1 2 3 4 5 6 7 8 9 10

Endorse yourself for your effort and any improvement!

EXAMPLE WORKSHEET

Step 1: Report a situation—an everyday event when you began to work yourself up. Describe what happened: specifically, what triggered temper and symptoms?

_____
_____
_____

Step 2: Report the symptoms you experienced—both physical and mental. (For instance, angry and fearful thoughts, confusion, tightness in your chest, low feelings, sweaty palms, and so on.)

_____
_____
_____

How would you rate your discomfort on a scale of 1 to 10? (1=mild through 10=very intense)

Before Spotting: 1 2 3 4 5 6 7 8 9 10

Step 3: Report your spotting of fearful and/or angry temper, the RI tools you used to help yourself, and self-endorsement for your effort.

_____
_____
_____
_____

Step 4: Describe what would have happened before your training—the reaction and discomfort you would have experienced—and rate your discomfort after spotting.

_____
_____
_____
_____

After Spotting: 1 2 3 4 5 6 7 8 9 10

Endorse yourself for your effort and any improvement!

EXAMPLE WORKSHEET

Step 1: Report a situation—an everyday event when you began to work yourself up. Describe what happened: specifically, what triggered temper and symptoms?

___

Step 2: Report the symptoms you experienced—both physical and mental. (For instance, angry and fearful thoughts, confusion, tightness in your chest, low feelings, sweaty palms, and so on.)

___

How would you rate your discomfort on a scale of 1 to 10? (1=mild through 10=very intense)

Before Spotting: 1 2 3 4 5 6 7 8 9 10

Step 3: Report your spotting of fearful and/or angry temper, the RI tools you used to help yourself, and self-endorsement for your effort.

___

Step 4: Describe what would have happened before your training—the reaction and discomfort you would have experienced—and rate your discomfort after spotting.

___

After Spotting: 1 2 3 4 5 6 7 8 9 10

Endorse yourself for your effort and any improvement!

Made in the USA
Monee, IL
10 September 2023